NORTHUMBRIAN NATURE DIARY

by

Wendy Dickson

Illustrations by John Steele

SANDHILL
PRESS

DEDICATION

In memory of my mother and father, Barbara and Reginald Dickson, both of whom took a keen interest in the natural world around them and helped and encouraged me to do likewise.

ACKNOWLEDGEMENTS

There are a number of people without whose help and encouragement this book would never have seen the light of day: particularly I am grateful to Keith Merrin and Andrew Bielinski of the Northumberland Wildlife Trust; Adrian Woodhall and John Walton of the National Trust; Bill Walker of the National Rivers Authority and Dr. Steve Percival of the University of Sunderland for their time and patience, to Tom Cadwallender of Druridge Bay Country Park for much friendly help and constructive comment and to his wife Muriel for her company on numerous field trips in all weathers; to Billy Shiel and his team for many enjoyable trips to the Farnes; to Peter Cruse of Alnwick Computerware for periodically saving me from maltreating my computer! I am greatly indebted to John Steele for the enormous amount of time and trouble he has devoted to the illustrations which so skilfully bring the text to life. Beryl Sanderson of the Sandhill Press has kindly and carefully nursed me through the complexities of book production. To them all I offer my sincere thanks. But mostly I am grateful to the subjects themselves which continually provide me with countless hours of pleasure and interest. Without them life would be very much poorer.

First published in Great Britain in 1993.
Sandhill Press Ltd.,
17 Castle St., Warkworth,
Morpeth, Northumberland, NE65 0UW.

Text © Wendy Dickson. Illustrations © John Steele.

Designed by Sandhill Press, set in Times 12pt, Italic.

ISBN 0 946098 31 X

Printed by Martins the Printers Ltd.

Northumbrian Nature Diary

JANUARY : *Retreating Reds*   Page   5

FEBRUARY : *Two Lovely Black Eyes*   10

MARCH : *Warts and All*   17

APRIL : *A Time of Yellow*   22

MAY : *A Cheviot Valley*   26

JUNE : *Nightime Manoeuvres*   31

JULY: *Muddy Masterpieces*   36

AUGUST : *Insect Miscellany*   42

SEPTEMBER : *On the Rocks*   46

OCTOBER : *Arctic Visitors*   52

NOVEMBER : *Pupping Time*   58

DECEMBER : *A Fishy Tale*   62

*J*ANUARY

RETREATING REDS

Red Alert! Red Alert! Something must be wrong. But what is it? To that there is no immediate answer though several people are actively seeking one.

Red refers to the red squirrel, and Alert to the fact that they are rapidly disappearing from the British countryside. Other than a few offshore islands, this part of north-east England is now one of their last mainland strongholds in Britain. But even here they are nowhere near as numerous as they once were. So just what is going wrong? With grey squirrels now beginning to creep into the county, the need to find that out takes on a new urgency.

In autumn 1991 the Wildlife Trusts of Northumberland, Durham & Cleveland, together with Museums North, set about seeking an answer. The Red Alert launch, which asked the public to send in all sightings of red squirrels to help accurately map their distribution, actually marked the beginning of a longer project to try and learn more about the way red squirrels live, what their needs are regarding habitat and resources, and to see if we need to give them a helping hand to make it through troubled times.

Mention squirrels to most people and they normally think of the grey; many have never had the privilege of seeing a red. Reds are rather smaller than greys, and in winter particularly have pronounced ear tufts. Otherwise, basically reds look red and greys look grey. Simple? Well, not always! Both species have different summer and winter coats, each being changed by moult. But when the red grows its reddish summer coat this is often covered with a surface of grey fur. Likewise, the grey in its summer coat, can be topped off with a reddish tinge. If you get a good view, you should be able to sort them out by their different shapes and sizes, but they don't always offer you that chance.

Apart from their looks, red and grey squirrels have another fundamental difference: the former are native to Britain, the latter are not. In 1876 two of these North Americans were introduced into Cheshire, starting a trend of similar introductions all over the country which began a whole new squirrel history in Britain.

Now people are very fond of saying that when the greys arrived from their assisted passage across the Atlantic, they set about driving the reds out, but this appears to be not altogether true. Greys can show aggression, but as much to their own kind as to reds. There is no direct evidence of actual fighting between species. Indeed, in some areas, reds have actually declined in advance of the greys arriving. It seems a little more complicated than that.

The history of red squirrels in Britain dates back to the last Ice Age between 7,000 and 10,000 years ago, they being one of the last mammals to arrive here before our land bridge with the continent disappeared under water, making us an island. Prior to that, fossil evidence has revealed the presence of a now extinct species of red squirrel in Britain dating back about 12,000 years. Our present-day red squirrels originally evolved in conifer forests, where they tend to live sparsely. But they do not exclusively occur in conifers.

In its native North America, however, broad-leaved woodland is where the more densely populated grey squirrel originates from, and in this country it seems likely that it does out-compete the red in this habitat. In the conifers, reds are well adapted to extract the seeds from small cones, but are less able to cope with the toxins that occur in acorns in broad-leaved woodland, whereas the greys find these no problem. Greys also tend to eat woodland fruits before they have ripened, whereas reds prefer their fruits ripe and juicy, but - alas - often find the cupboard is bare by then.

One surprising factor about squirrels is that if they are going to succumb to starvation, it will not be in the depths of winter as you might predict, but rather in the depths of summer when all might seem well. Winter provides many natural food sources in the form of nuts and fruits, spring throws up much new growth of shoots and seeds, but summer ...

To go out specifically to look for red squirrels can be a frustrating experience. Red squirrels will cross your path when it suits them and not when it suits you. But if you keep your eyes open as you walk around suitable wooded habitat, you may well be lucky. Tucked motionless in the fork of a Scots Pine 4 to 5 metres up, tail seductively curled round, they look little different from the reddish colour of that tree's trunk. But a couple scampering after each other on the woodland floor gives you a more memorable view.

Of course there are places where you have a better chance of catching up with them: Wallington Hall for instance or Bolam Lake. But one turned up on a bird table in Alnmouth a few years ago, and whichever way it got there, it must have travelled a fair distance over open country, and maybe a bit of water, to arrive! Squirrels can swim, though I have never seen one do so.

Failing a successful sighting, you can, of course, help yourself by finding clues to their presence. A good search of a woodland floor may produce the distinctive chewed pine cones often with just the centre stem left, that are one of the hallmarks of a red squirrel. While up above you might notice a drey tucked in the fork of a tree or close in against the trunk - one of several that may be used by an individual animal. They are more obvious in winter before the tree foliage hides them, and probably provide good shelter in inclement weather conditions. Returning later to places of obvious activity may well reward you.

Red squirrels are active in winter, specifically during the early part of the year, when males are busy chasing females. As they rove in search of the opposite sex, it is at this time of year that several of them fall victim to cars on the roads. I myself have to stand in the guilty corner as having but once killed one near Cragside. A terrible feeling of helplessness overtook me as I watched the accident unfold but could take no sensible action to avoid the tragedy. In fact, deaths on roads account for more corpses than do predators.

Other mistakes that they make are not necessarily fatal. In Alnwick's Hulne Park one winter, I encountered six red squirrels around Brizlee Tower, one of which was actually climbing up the stone folly itself, presumably in the mistaken belief that it was a tree! When I came upon it, so it ascended further, and I felt duty bound to hasten my exit in case one false move on its part meant it descending rather quicker than planned! In any case, coming down would be a slightly more difficult operation than going up, though they can rotate their hind feet through 180 degrees to enable them to hang on tight at the rear end!

Diseases do not appear to be a major problem and there is as yet no evidence that those experienced by one species are passed on to the other. They also have their own specific species of fleas to keep them company but which they do not share. Predators do *not seem to be a major problem; cats are probably the main, but not a serious, one, though one lady, suspecting her own moggy of killing them, actually turned the tables on him instead! Drastic action. A few probably fall prey to hawks.*

So just what can we do to help the red squirrel? Well, researchers are now fitting radio collars to a few individuals so that they can be tracked through the more private parts of their lives. One interesting fact that has so far emerged from this is that they apparently prefer feeding on the smaller seeds of Lodgepole Pine and Norway Spruce, to the almost total exclusion of the larger Sitka Spruce seeds. However, it is much too early to say whether this is normal, or just a one-off situation. Certainly the more we learn about their daily lives and requirements, the more it may be possible to manipulate certain conditions to help them.

As for the greys, well no-one is standing at the border with muzzles loaded waiting to repel raiders. By 1992, as a result of the Red Alert campaign, there were already two confirmed reports of grey squirrels in two widely separated areas in the west of the county. But by the time they get here in any numbers, we may be in a much better position to give the reds a helping hand. To those who say we should leave them all to their own devices, the sad fact is that, due to centuries of human influence on the countryside, very little of our wildlife is 'wild' these days and it is up to us to try and make good the bad that has gone before.

In the first instance, Red Alert only lasted six months, but in the following winters the general public is again being asked to get involved with reporting red squirrels. So keep your eyes open and your notebooks ready, for you could be making a vital contribution to the red squirrel's future in Northumberland. It would be a sad day if we lost these delightful creatures as part of our wildlife heritage in Northumberland.

*F*EBRUARY

TWO LOVELY BLACK EYES

Winter. Snow on the ground. For more than a week the wind has been blowing from the east, veering from south-east through to north-east, and bringing an icy blast and frequent fresh snowfalls from the continent. It has also brought birds with it, escaping from the intensely cold temperatures to the east and north. Rough seas have thrown a large ration of dead and dying auks onto the beach, emaciated from impossible feeding conditions in heavy seas.

Out on the lake, tucked in behind the dunes, things are marginally easier, though part of it freezes over on several nights. Between the snowstorms which temporarily obliterate the scene, wildfowl are seen in discreet groups, interspersed with pale gulls that have a frosted look about them, and dark coots. A quick scan reveals some mallard, floating rafts of pochard distinctively hunched up, red heads tucked into grey backs, while among them smaller and rather more lively black and white male tufted ducks dive alongside their browner females.

This is Druridge Bay Country Park, encompassing Ladyburn Lake which itself has variously been known in the past as Coldrife Pool and Hadston Lake and which was originally created out of a previous opencast site. The Country Park itself, owned and run by Northumberland County Council, and with two full-time wardens and a well-appointed visitor centre, was opened in 1989. Having stickleback, minnows and eels in it, the lake is quite a magnet for wintering wildfowl, particularly diving ducks, and is rapidly gaining a reputation for unusual and interesting birds.

Moving out to scan the lake more thoroughly, the binoculars suddenly focus upon a little circle of ripples radiating outwards. Something has just dived. Instinctively watching the very spot, the wait seems endless. But luck is in and right in view a small bundle of feathers plops to the surface. Initial surprise turns to pleasure when it reveals itself as a male smew ... a handsome bird indeed and member of a handsome family of half a dozen species which stretches across the old and new world. They are known collectively as 'sawbills', due to the serrated edges of their long thin mandibles which enable them to catch, hold and swallow, their fish diet.

Of the three species occurring in Europe including Britain, Ladyburn Lake is one of the few places in the country where in winter you can sometimes see all three together. For, in addition to a few smew, rather more red-breasted mergansers - sometimes over sixty - pass that period of the year here, while more occasional visits from the largest member of the group - the goosander - periodically completes the trio. Of the three, the males of each are strikingly different, while a definite theme with various permutations runs through the females; that of greyish bodies and coppery red heads. All are crested to greater or lesser degree and are the epitome of wildness.

February is the time when wildfowl are looking at their very best, prior to the onset of the breeding season, and the colourful male sawbills are no exception. Male goosanders - almost goose-like as their name suggests - have dark green heads and backs, with a wonderful pink glow to the pale breast and underparts.

Male mergansers, for their part are a veritable tapestry of colours - dark green heads held up by white clerical collars, umber patterning on the breast leading back towards black and white shoulder pads, and completed by dark upperparts, white wing flashes and greyish body, beginning and ending with red bill and legs. Furthermore, they disport themselves on the water with an air to match their finery.

But arguably the most special member of the group is the smew; it is also the smallest as indeed its name may suggest, smew probably being an old word for small, though some think it may be an abbreviation for 'sea mew'.

While the female is striking in her own way, with distinctive white cheeks standing out prominently against her coppery head and hindneck, and responsible for the old Northumbrian name of weasel duck for the obvious likeness of her features to that creature, the male is quite different, so different in fact that perhaps not surprisingly some of our forefather ornithologists thought male and female belonged to two entirely different species.

His plumage is mainly white, but what raises his profile above other white birds is that his is delicately etched with black tracery blending into gentler vermiculations on his flanks. He exudes an aura of icy wastes. From the rear, a delicate black outline highlights the white crest that runs back from his forehead. But as he turns to face you, you get an almost startling view and one that the books never show you: that of two large eyes looking out through a dramatic black mask - truly an avian highwayman. In flight he changes to a darker looking bird for his open wing shows more black than white, creating a noticeable character change!

The main European wintering grounds for smew are in Holland where several thousand may occur, but each winter, depending on the weather, a few hundred fly to spend this inclement part of the year in Britain, females and young males predominating in the south, with a scattering elsewhere. Ladyburn Lake seems favoured, but they will also move onto the adjacent reserves of the Northumberland Wildlife Trust along the bay - Hauxley to the north, Druridge Pools and Cresswell Pond to the south.

In one recent winter six adult males were present on the lake for a few short hours with four females, but I have never had the good fortune to see more than one adult male at a time. One of my strangest sightings of smew was a number of years ago at Blagdon Lake near Bristol, where an adult male was keeping company with an almost totally albino coot that retained just a smattering of normal black feathers in its plumage; the two formed an unusual and somewhat confusing spectacle! Smew characteristically do not mix much with other species.

In some years, a male that was born the previous summer may spend the winter with us. When he arrives, often about November-time, he looks to all intents and purposes like the female, as do many other first-winter drakes at this time. Female and early first-winter sawbills are known as redheads. But as winter wears on, he will gradually lose his juvenile plumage and start to acquire his adult feathering, becoming noticeably paler and soon getting his black mask. By his second winter he will be in fully adult plumage. The males are not resplendent just for our pleasure; it is for the serious business of courtship that must get under way.

The wind has veered round to the north-east. On the lake a group of four mergansers are getting their spiky crests blown up over their heads as they briefly turn their backs to the wind. There are three males and a female. Swimming in rough circles, the three males suddenly start displaying to the female. Communal courtship is not uncommon among these birds and in places where greater numbers occur, it can involve large groups.

Throwing their heads up, beaks pointing skywards, the neck and head are suddenly flattened along the water surface, with bill open and pointing vertically. Simultaneously the back is humped up, the tail pressed down. It all looks awkward and uncomfortable, but only lasts momentarily and is designed to show off their best features to the female. For her part she looks somewhat unconcerned while all this is happening, but then falls in behind one of the males as the group separate out. Not to be spurned so easily, the other two males turn and follow in hot pursuit, with more displaying.

But clearly vanquished for the present, they move off to a quiet part and begin a prolonged preening session, not, as we might like to think, to consciously spruce themselves up to look smarter for the next bout of display, for that is a human sentiment, but rather to keep their plumage in general good condition as this is vitally important for their everyday existence; unkempt feathers hamper flight and hinder insulation, unoiled plumage leads to waterlogging and thus chilling. So the bill is frequently rubbed against the oil gland just above the tail, body feathers are communally oiled, wing feathers are individually passed through the bill and simultaneously 're-zipped' as it were, each little component barbule being hooked back onto the one next door to keep it working efficiently. Mergansers rarely breed in Northumberland so these birds will be leaving soon to return to their breeding grounds further north and need their plumage in tip-top condition to undertake the journey. Goosanders on the other hand breed fairly extensively in the county, but the main Northumbrian wintering concentrations are away from the Park.

Smew too are thinking about spring. Their breeding grounds are some way from Britain, covering a small part of northern Scandinavia and a large part of northern and eastern Russia in the vast open spaces of the taiga. While smew display is perhaps a little more muted than that of the mergansers, it still involves throwing the head back, puffing out the chest and sometimes even rising vertically in the water. Occasionally the male will turn his head away showing off his black-lined crest. Pairing usually takes place before they get to the breeding grounds, either on the wintering area or during the migration flight back.

I manage to catch up with three at Druridge Pools at the end of February, after much rain runoff has apparently driven them off the muddied waters of the Park. Here one male has two females to display to. When I arrive these females are at the far side of the pool, but they are moving towards the male, diving continuously as they go, until they catch up with him in a little bay. He swims away, they follow in single file, but as he turns to face them so the roles are reversed and they scuttle away ahead of him. It is a miserable cold misty day, with a persistent moderate wind blowing in off the sea, ruffling his crest as he turns! He lets them go and preens, but later joins up with them and just as he approaches one he dives right underneath her and surfaces beyond! Then he throws his head back a couple of times. But all this seems not to impress them. It all fizzles out and they split up again. There is time yet.

The females then join a group of goldeneyes, one of the few species wintering smew will mix with. These big-headed diving ducks breed sparingly in Scotland but mainly further north and east, spending the remainder of the year throughout most of Britain and the continent in a variety of habitats, being equally at home on the sea as on freshwater lakes or rivers. Although not sawbills, they are closely related and where their breeding areas overlap with smew, the two may occasionally hybridise.

Smew and goldeneye, along with goosanders, nest above the ground in tree holes, but will readily take to nestboxes in the right areas. When the ducklings hatch, they merely flutter down to the ground in their first few hours, their lightness of weight saving them from what seems like certain injury.

With the onset of March the sawbills are becoming restless and harder to see, as the urge to move northwards grows. During the month most of the wildfowl will leave Ladyburn Lake and the adjacent reserves to start the sometimes long trek back to the breeding areas. Only a handful of mallard and the occasional pair of shelduck will keep the mute swans company during the summer months, when the lake is utilised by human visitors for water sports. The sawbills and their companions will return in the autumn, and who knows, next winter might be the one when I see more than just two lovely black eyes peering at me from the lake! The prospect is exciting.

Mᴀʀᴄʜ

WARTS AND ALL

     While grey foggy days and iced-over ponds may not convince us that winter will soon be over, for some creatures this is the most important and feverish time of year. Having spent the past few months hibernating, in the early part of the year they awaken and proceed to make their way down to a pond. For these animals are toads and, along with their first-cousins, frogs, the over-riding urge is on to mate and spawn and create the next generation.

Winter for the toads will have been spent in some secluded situation, maybe under a pile of stones or a piece of wood, perhaps even underground. Through choice, damp places are avoided in favour of dry ones. When the spring temperature hits a critical 5°-6°C, however, they will awaken and leave their hibernaculum to make off to the breeding pond at full speed - relatively speaking! Other factors play their part: mild moist weather seems to be an encouragement. Most travelling is done at night; in nature this has advantages; in our modern society it throws up disadvantages too.

One such favoured spawning site for toads is the marsh beside Alnmouth Village golf course. On two sides it is surrounded by dense vegetation - the old woody stems of last year's willowherbs, long grass, clumps of bramble and other shrubbery; on the third side is the village and in the remaining corner is that formidable barrier, the North Sea. Yet the toads appear from most directions and somehow make their way through what to them must seem like an overgrown jungle. Built more for walking than for hopping, they steadfastly plod on, down from the hill, out from some surrounding gardens, and across the road. And it is in crossing the road that we come onto the scene.

For toads crossing the road do so with frequent stops: in our car headlights a pausing toad bears a remarkable resemblance to a small pile of mud and as such we tend to ignore it. But the legacy of our misjudgements lies in the cold light of dawn with the several flattened corpses littering the tarmac. The carnage is a sorry sight.

Toads are tremendously traditional in returning to their ancestral ponds each year, and in the interim, to suit our needs but oblivious to theirs, roads may be built along the route. In extreme cases the pond itself may even have been drained, or the returning toads may find that a new housing estate with all its attendant hazards has been built where once was home.

At a spawning pond in the north of the county, the North Northumberland Bird Club have enterprisingly extended their interest from things feathered to things cold and warty as well and for the appropriate few weeks during March and early April, have gained the necessary authority in conjunction with the Northumberland Wildlife Trust to erect temporary but official toad crossing road signs to warn motorists of the hazard.

At Alnmouth the toads don't yet have the benefit of officialdom but they do have the burgesses on their side who themselves erect warning signs of the dangers, and periodically give some of them a helping hand across the road. Helping toads across the road does not appeal to everyone. Their cold and rather warty skins may feel unpleasant, and the toads themselves do not always appreciate being picked up and will wriggle and squirm a good deal. But helping them survive in an increasingly hostile world is a deed well done.

Toads may come from quite a distance, sometimes up to a mile. How they actually find the pond is not known, maybe there is a special scent they are sensitive to - could it be just memory? Whatever, there are nonetheless numerous obstacles to overcome on the way. At Alnmouth, for instance, having safely negotiated the highway, there is then the kerbstone to be mastered - sometimes twice their height. I watched one walking along the bottom of this barrier for a short way when it came to a clod of earth and grass leaning up against the kerb; it promptly clambered up this 'mounting block' and over the top and that problem was solved. But the most amazing feat to me is their negotiation of a way through all the vegetation, which to my eyes looks totally impenetrable. But from a toad's viewpoint there is a way through; there must be.

For a number of females, sometimes the majority, the journey is made doubly hard for, if a male meets up with one on the way, he promptly clambers aboard and hitches *a lift all the rest of the way to the pond! He will put his front legs round underneath hers in what is known as amplexus and she has to carry him across roads, over kerbstones and other obstacles and through the vegetation. Relief for her is not at hand until spawning is finished, though, unlike frogs, toads already paired usually start spawning as soon as they reach the breeding pond rather than waiting around for the majority of others to arrive.*

Toads tend to prefer rather deeper water than frogs and will continue spawning during the day as well as at night, unless cold weather overtakes them. The female lays her eggs in strings. Naturally this takes rather longer to achieve than frogs that lay their spawn in more casual clumps which float to the surface. The male toad now has to do a bit of work in return for his free passage to the pond. With the tips of his back legs, he can sense when the eggs are being laid, and then fertilise them. Although the female stops for a rest quite frequently (she must by now be utterly exhausted), the pair are nevertheless still attached to the spawn string until laying is completed. The end result is a ribbon of spawn sometimes almost as much as 3 metres long which is wound round the underwater stems of plants.

Toads seem to have good eyesight, though how far they can see and what sort of image they behold is not fully known. Walking along the road, one that was sitting in the grass on the adjacent verge moved as soon as it perceived me stop to look at it. Most but by no means all move under cover of darkness hauling up by day in long grass or rank vegetation.

An added problem for one individual came to light when I found it in long grass beside the golf course and close to, but not in, the pond. A dog being exercised came over to investigate me, ignoring for as long as it dared its master's calls. When it did decide it was time for obedience, it promptly trod on the toad beside me, and while on this occasion shock seemed to be the worst result, big sharp claws could well lacerate skin and perhaps introduce disease.

Finding toadspawn in the water is not so easy and not really to be recommended for in plodging round looking for it you may unwittingly squash other toads that have not yet left the water. Once spawning is finished, the toads disperse individually, their chief objective over for another year. That marks the end of this year's commitment towards the next generation; once the tadpoles hatch, they are on their own! And the odds will be stacked heavily against them. They represent a good banquet for several predators that share their early world, though they are less palatable than frog tadpoles.

By midsummer, they are usually undergoing their metamorphosis from tadpole to tiny toadlet; their tails will not finally disappear until they are out on dry land. Those that survive the terrestrial predators ready to gulp them up once they leave the water, often during a downpour of rain, will disperse to start growing into adults. Toads probably don't breed until two or three years old; in the interim there are many risks to run. But they can defend themselves well by blowing themselves up to look extra formidable to predators, and also, when under severe pressure, by secreting a white sticky and somewhat poisonous substance through the skin which obviously tastes really unpleasant to any animal unwise enough to try and take a bite.

And next year ... well, it will all happen again, with the first-time breeders integrating with the old hands. It's worth spending a few damp nights out there watching them foregathering, and you might be able to do a little toad transporting also! But be careful where you tread!

APRIL

A $TIME$ OF $YELLOW$

April brings with it the promise of spring - sometimes a delayed promise as we sit and shiver in easterly gales or even get dusted with snow - but a promise nonetheless. Even earlier in the year the signs are there - buds forming on trees and shrubs, leaves pushing up through the sometimes sodden soil. Identifying them can be quite a challenge, but there are familiar faces among them. It is an exciting time of the year. It is the herald for a time of yellow.

April is usually escorted in by coltsfoot still in flower; in an early spring it is even past its best. Its sulphur yellow flowers glow from dunes and ditches, embankments and forgotten places. It is the "son-before-father" of our ancestors, for the scaly leaves that clasp the flowering stem are only a forerunner of the real thing.

But those real leaves, the shape of which give the plant its common name, can fool us for, coming as they do after most of the flowers have died down, they do not conveniently associate themselves with this same plant.

The down on the underside of these distinctive leaves was at one time put to good use being scraped off for firelighting tinder. But surely more importantly the whole leaves were dried and placed in pipes, the smoking of which was said to form relief from asthma, while their juice was put to curing coughs, accounting for the plant's scientific name of Tussilago. A pity some of these remedies have passed out of common usage.

As coltsfoot fades for another year, so other blooms are rising up for opening time between the shiny heart-shaped leaves of lesser celandine.

Essentially at home on the woodland floor, this plant spreads itself over a variety of other habitats and its upwards of eight bright yellow petals betray its allegiance to the buttercup family. It keeps its head down for the gales that can sweep across country at this time may play havoc with its beauty.

In other parts of the woodland, along the hedgerows and grassy banks, the more delicately shaded primrose is also showing itself, a favourite of many and perhaps more familiar than the celandine.

Primroses produce two kinds of flower, and in order for them to become fertilised,

pollen from one kind needs to be transferred to the other - not a complicated operation, you might think, but even Shakespeare noted that they flower when not many insects are around and chronicled this fact in 'The Winter's Tale' with a delightfully unscientific phrase: "pale primroses that die unmarried". Thus some go unpollinated.

But a close relative of the primrose is steadily growing up in the world during April, not in woodland but more on the short-cropped turf behind the dunes and other grassland areas: the cowslip. The somewhat wrinkly leaves forming a rosette are showing well as the month comes in and in some places even the flower stems are over an inch high, but the range in timing perhaps partly depends on how late into the spring the turf is grazed by stock. Those at Druridge Bay and Boulmer seem to be about two weeks behind those further north at Newton Links - no matter for we can enjoy them all the longer.

As the flowerheads grow and open out, they present a crown of yellow towards the end of the month, nodding gently in the breeze. This arrangement gave rise to the legend surrounding another name for this plant -the "bunch of keys". It was said that when St. Peter discovered a second set of keys to the gates of Heaven, he dropped his own set immediately; where they landed was the spot that the first cowslip sprang up. "Paigle" also derives from this source. St. Peter did us proud with this legacy. But what of the name "cowslip"? Well, that may come from the fact that people always associated it with growing close by a cow 'slop' or cowpat!

Like its relative the primrose, the cowslip also has two types of flower - 'pin' and 'thrum'. But coming into bloom a little later than the primrose, there are more insects at large and those with long tongues such as some bees and moths visit both sorts of flower and unwittingly undertake the operation of pollination. The stamens are positioned such on the one type that they cause the pollen to attach itself to the topside of the insects' tongues, and thus it is at exactly the right height to reach the stigma on the other type of flower when that is visited. Of course, it doesn't always work, but pretty often judging by the increased amount of cowslip flowers each year!

Here in Northumberland we are fortunate to have a wonderful display of cowslips along the coast as well as inland. Those just north of Newton Haven, flowering as they do up to the top of the bank, brighten many a coastal walk. At one time, their beauty was their demise, as many people uprooted the plants to relocate them in their gardens. Happily this is now against the law, and the cowslips have spread to a number of new sites, in appreciation of their new-found protection.

They will continue to flower from the second half of April, through May and well into June, by which time other flowers on the dunes have sprung up to join them including that other yellow delight, bird's foot trefoil, more appositely referred to perhaps as eggs and bacon, the 'bacon' being the streaky effect of the buds before they open out to become the 'eggs'! All these against the brilliant yellow background of the pungent flowering gorse.

But pinks and reds and whites and blues in various combinations are also now appearing to give some variety to the countryside. These alternatives are also beautiful in their own individual ways and are a welcome addition as we move on towards the next season of the year, but they do herald the fact that the 'time of yellow' is coming to an end for another year. It was welcome while it lasted.

M_{AY}

A CHEVIOT VALLEY

When I lived in Bristol and worked in the BBC Natural History Unit Sound Library, I noticed the location for several recordings of birds read 'Harthope Valley, Northumberland'. I suppose it was 'Northumberland' that caught my eye for at that time part of my family were already living in the county. But the name 'Harthope' excited my imagination. One day, perhaps ...

The first time I crept over the crown of the hill at Skirl Naked, nothing had quite prepared me for the view that beckoned me. It was so different from anything I had ever seen before - a yawning gap within the surrounding hills. I had to go on. It was early summer and the gorse was in full flower. Gently edging my way along the narrow road down to the floor of the valley, the more I saw the more it took a hold on me. To this day, my love of the place grows with every subsequent visit.

Created by a fortunate fault of geology ions ago in time and subsequently ground down and rounded off during the Ice Age by ice moving down from neighbouring Cheviot, its most noticeable feature nowadays also has its source in the foothills of the Cheviots in the shape of the Harthope Burn. This lively piece of water, swelled by various smaller burns along its route, bubbles and splashes its way down through the valley to join up with the Carey Burn at the north-east end; subsequently this combination flows on down through Happy Valley before turning north to become Wooler Water.

At this time of year the resident dippers are most obvious, standing defiantly on a mid-stream boulder with a beakful of caddis and mayfly larvae, waiting until your back is momentarily turned before flying up to the nest to feed a growing family. Further downstream the neighbouring pair already have their young out and about - drabber versions of their parents with a rather scaly appearance, but with the characteristic bobbing action from which their name is derived.

During April and May, the dippers are joined on their stretch of fast-flowing water by several other birds - common sandpipers that have recently returned from their winter sojourn in Africa, which now grace the burn with their attractive wing-raising displays; gaudy oystercatchers up from the coast which, despite their appearances, blend in remarkably well with their surroundings; and delightful and dainty grey wagtails flirting their long tails as they move from boulder to boulder or land on an overhanging alder branch.

The strength of the Harthope Valley, however, lies in its many different habitats. Where else in a day could you find the wild creatures typical of fast-flowing streams with their surrounding haughlands, woodland, moorland and high tops in such close proximity? Here, it is all together.

In summer, I often spend several hours walking the lower hillsides of the valley searching for a rather special reptile that can be found here - the adder. Not that adders are the sort of creatures that everyone wishes to seek out, which is just as well for the adders!

Our only poisonous snake, and in fact one of only three species that we have in Britain, adders spend the winter in hibernation, and it is when they first emerge in spring that they are still rather dozy and therefore unlikely to move out of the way if danger threatens. What these cold-blooded creatures need most on these initial spring appearances is the rays of the sun to warm them up and make them more lively. Likewise in autumn, with the shortening days becoming cooler, they again become lethargic as they try to soak up the last of the sun's heat before retreating down some old rodent burrow or other suitable frost-free site for their winter hibernation.

Although their vision is probably reasonable, they are unable to hear in the same way as we can, for they possess neither an outer ear nor an eardrum. The only method they have of detecting approaching danger is by picking up vibrations that can reach their inner ear by way of their lower jawbone. Their most highly developed sense is that of smell, though again unlike us they do not pick up smells through a nose but rather through the tongue. Hence the familiar image of a snake flicking its tongue in and out; this is sampling the air to sort out smells and when it is seeking out a meal, the tongue works fast to gather information more quickly for processing by the pursuing snake.

Snakes unfortunately have a bad reputation, caused in large part by our lack of understanding of the lifestyles of these highly sophisticated creatures. In reality they are quite shy and on the odd occasion when we do have a bad experience with them, we should perhaps bear in mind that like us they are only trying to defend themselves from danger and are not seeking a confrontation; they would, in fact, much rather avoid one. Sadly - and perhaps surprisingly - some people try to catch them or provoke them into attack, when they should rather be treated with the greatest respect.

Adders tend to be traditional in their basking sites which are usually situated in a fairly sheltered position where the maximum amount of sun is available. I remember, a number of years ago, visiting a site in southern England early in the season when about a dozen were all congregated on the same grassy slope; it was a memorable experience. To get close to them, you need to move slowly and quietly, or they will detect the vibrations of your footfall and slip away into cover before you have seen them properly. The Harthope Valley is an ideal spot for them with grassy banks and patches of bracken interspersed with short-cropped sheep walks.

The males usually appear first in spring; with their often highly coloured bold zigzag striping extending down the entire length of the body, rather than making them more obvious, it actually helps to break up their outline against their randomly patterned backgrounds. A good view may also reveal the V-shaped mark on the back of the head, though I do not find this feature that easy to see. Females tend to emerge a few weeks later; they are generally rather more subtly coloured than the males against which mature females are also larger, though rarely exceed more than about 60 cm. Reaching sexual maturity when they are between two and three years old, courtship and mating take place soon after they come out of hibernation, and in late summer the females give birth to maybe up to a dozen live young which measure up to 15 to 20 cm. long. They stay close to their mother for the first few vulnerable days, even though they are quite capable of fending for themselves and already able to inflict a poisonous bite if necessary.

By late autumn they will have disappeared along with the other creatures that use this beautiful valley for the summer months of their lives. The whole area will become quieter in winter; the hills will take on a bleaker aspect, the burn a colder temperature as the first snowfalls of winter start to fall. The adders will be safely underground, sometimes in communal hibernating sites and occasionally right alongside those creatures that in summer they hunt; now they are oblivious to the elements on the surface, but, along with the sandpipers and the wagtails who beat the winter in different ways, they will reappear next spring to add to the quality of this unique Cheviot valley.

*J*UNE

NIGHTIME MANOEUVRES

There is something mysterious about creatures that inhabit our night-time world. Looking eery in the gathering gloom, they play on our imagination, and we are a trifle insecure when they come close to us as they are suddenly there, flitting silently around you before disappearing whence they came. It forms the recipe for superstition.

We need have no fears. These silent hunters are bats and the bats we have in this country are all perfectly harmless, with no desire to get tangled up in our hair. While they may be curious and come close to us to get a better look, from which habit the myth no doubt arose, we are merely objects to be avoided for they are more interested in the insects flying above our heads.

One summer evening as darkness started to evict the remaining daylight, a group of us assembled under the watchful guidance of some members of the Northumberland Bat Group, beside an imposing priory alongside the River Coquet, where once monks quietly went about their devotions. From under the eaves of this majestic building, used by bats for their summer roost site, the first ones would soon start to emerge.

Bats are, of course - flying mammals. They have a warm covering of fur over most of their bodies but the wings that enable them to get airborne resemble our hands, the bony fingers of which have a thin membranous covering going right across them and enclosing the hind legs down as far as the foot and including the tail as well.

With the aid of modern technology in the form of a bat detector, we were able to pick up the high frequency sounds made by the bats from within the building as they started to jostle around the exit point waiting for the first one to go forth. The ultrasonic sounds that bats make are usually inaudible to our ears; we cannot tune in to their high frequency. Therefore, we have to cheat by using machinery that can 'translate' the sounds for us at our own level.

Suddenly it happened: the first bat came out and there was a little excited gasp from its admirers. The idea was to count them as they emerged, but the darker it got the less sure you could be in your mind that the bat you had just seen had actually come out of the roost site and not flown a circle and returned over the roof! That is one of the hazards of the job. At this particular site there is not only more than one exit, there is more than one kind of bat as well!

Northumberland, in its northern setting, can only boast eight bat species on its records out of a total of fifteen in Britain as a whole, though several of these are becoming distinctly rare if not extinct nationally, and the total may well be only fourteen, perhaps even thirteen, by now. Of our eight, the pipistrelle has the dubious distinction of being the commonest; here there is just a small roost of males. One of our smallest bats, they share this particular roost during the summer with a slightly larger species, Daubenton's bat.

Until a few years ago, these were the only two kinds of bats known to use this summer roost, but then it was discovered one evening that some of the bats emerging were different: Natterer's bats, an exciting 'reward' for the dedicated Bat Group workers.

My particular interest was in the Daubenton's bats, the alternative name for this attractive creature being the water bat. Named after a French naturalist, they return to this summer roost site any time after the middle of April, and usually stay until August during which time they give birth to their single young. At the end of the summer they probably move to their winter hibernation site, but where that is still remains a mystery. Being adjacent to the River Coquet, when they emerge from the priory eaves they make their way down to the river to seek out the night's offerings of water-loving insects.

We followed them down and, with the aid of a powerful torch beam, could actually pick them out as they zoomed over the water surface, resembling miniature hovercraft. It was also possible, at times, to pick up others flying somewhat higher; these were possibly pipistrelles.

Daubenton's bats are able to travel at between ten and fifteen miles per hour, and may range as far as a mile from the roost, though one is said to havegone almost six times as far, no mean feat for so small a creature. As they go so they scoop up insects in the membranous pocket surrounding the tail before transferring it to the mouth.

Many of the insects they catch are pest species, and bats take plenty of them: for instance, it has been estimated that one hundred pipistrelles can account for 9 million midges in a month! Daubenton's bats will take water-haunting insects like caddis flies in flight, but will sometimes pick an insect directly off the water surface/

Although bats have eyes with which they can see quite well, thus confounding the saying "Blind as a Bat", it is during hunting, particularly, that their sophisticated ultrasonic echo-location system really comes into its own, for it not only helps them to find their way around during the hours of darkness, but additionally helps them locate their prey. Very simply, it works by the bats emitting frequent short sharp shouts and then listening to see how long they take to bounce back off solid objects around.

By also taking into account the different patterns of sound and maybe the different directions from which they return, the creature can also detect a moving object, say one of those nourishing midges. Thus they serve to give the bat a mental picture of its surroundings - clever stuff, eh?   Each different species of bat has a different speed and pattern of calls - Daubenton's gives out a rather fast and regular pattern of clicks that has been timed at about thirteen to the second.

Although we are usually unable to hear the bats, they can at times hear us for there are certain ultrasonic elements in our own speech and in the sounds we make in moving around that, if they become too frequent, can disturb roosting bats.   Although they are strictly protected by law, in large part for their specialised roosting requirements, many populations are, nevertheless, declining rapidly and there is still so much we do not know about them.

Here on the banks of the Coquet, where many generations ago the Augustinian monks probably noticed these flitting forms as they padded softly to their prayers, they are now well protected by English Heritage, and well monitored by the Northumberland Bat Group who hope that by adding to our knowledge of these delightful creatures through their painstaking work they can not only give bats the better reputation they deserve but a better and more secure future also.

*J*ULY

MUDDY MASTERPIECES

Walking south along the seaward edge of the links from Craster, the coastal contour shortly turns westwards at a right angle to form the dramatic dolerite cliffs of Cullernose Point. At this time of year, long before you get there, as often as not you will hear a cacophony of avian cadences as birds rise and fall from view around the cliff face. But as you turn the corner and climb the gentle incline, the full panorama of a busy seabird colony is set out before you.

The main species of seabird to inhabit these cliffs is the kittiwake, one of our smallest, and surely our most elegant, gull. Not only that, but just in case you are in any doubt, the adults periodically break out into a series of calls to remind you of why they have that name: "kittiwaak, kittiwaak", which echoes round the half circle of rocks.

Gentle in expression, immaculate in plumage, sociable in nature, the kittiwakes here are annually expanding their colony southwards along the available ledges. It never fails to amaze how the smallest apology for a ledge can be put to good use topped off with a nest of grassy vegetation stuck down with guano to protect the growing young.

In July these young are, to my mind, looking at their very best as they sport the dramatic black markings of a half neck-collar and broken inverted 'W' across the wings against the background of blue-grey plumage with white face and underparts. For my money a young kittiwake would take a handsome prize for beauty.

Interspersed among them, and shown up by the kittiwake's 'clean' look, fulmar petrels patrol the cliffs in their ever inquisitive fashion, passing close by the observer on stiff wings as their dark eyes watch you.

Their 'white' parts are more creamy, their 'grey' wings patterned and flecked with browns, causing their far less pristine appearance. They have young in the nest too, ugly fat offspring changing from their downy plumage into one more like their parents.

Fortunately here they are out of reach of observers, for too close an approach to one of them will be met by a volume of abuse in the form of a vomit of its most recent meal, almost certainly fish offal parcelled up in oil, spewed out with deadly accuracy.

They are best left well alone. Some have adults sitting alongside them on the bare earth that suffices for a nest, *other patches have pairs of adults that may in fact not have bred at all; fulmars are long-lived birds that do not start breeding until they are about nine years old, but may well go through the motions before then. Every now and again one of these pairs will let out their cackling calls as they twist and shake their heads at each other like dancing cobras in a courtship display. Fulmars are great cacklers.*

But as you continue south along the cliff path a very different sound meets your ears, a pleasant twittering, much quieter and more musical than the other sounds and not one typical of seabirds at all. That is not surprising for the perpetrators of these are none other than house martins, birds that you might well be surprised to find along the cliff edge.

However this place supports quite a sizeable cliff-nesting colony of these birds; in the recent past up to 140 nests have been counted while in 1990, the total was 78 nests. Numbers in any colony, however, are known to fluctuate annually.

Long before bricks and mortar became the fashion, house martins naturally used the available places on a rocky face to build their nests, constructing their masterpieces of muddy masonry under the rocky overhangs. Nowadays natural cliff sites are much less common as the birds have, as their very name suggests, happily adapted to the convenient situations that our buildings provide. With a variety to choose from in Northumberland, nest sites have included an old railway bridge and inside a lime kiln!

Depending on how early or late the spring is which will often dictate their arrival time, the parent house martins are busy feeding their offspring about the second half of July. Walking under the cliffs you can see several nests with the nearly fledged young peering perilously out through the narrow entrance which is right up against the overhanging cliff. They watch every move until they hear and see their parents returning with a beakful of insects. The adults have perhaps gleaned their spoils from high in the sky right above their nest, or have perhaps had to travel further afield to satisfy their hungry offspring. This matters little to these young whose only interest at that moment is another meal.

They lean out as far as they dare calling in excitement as the parent lands, perhaps just on the edge of the nest cup, to pass the food in, or frequently entering themselves, probably to undertake a little nest sanitation at the same time.

But while one family is being stuffed full of nutrition in preparation for that all-important first flight, just along the cliff another pair are rebuilding a nest that appears not to have been used so far this season. House martins are frequently double-brooded and while many nests are re-used in the same season, one benefit of using a new nest for the second brood is that it escapes any parasites that may have taken up residence within the nest cup. Other pairs are also repairing nests; these may be latecomers - maybe first-time breeders - who have not so far raised a family at all this year.

Whatever the reason and the requirement, it is fascinating to watch the birds return with wet mud and gradually build up the broken wall of the nest. Progress can be followed quite easily as the newly placed dark pellets of fresh mud take a while to dry in much the same way as does wet cement on a new house wall.

The building materials are normally collected within about 100 metres of the nest; in dry years house martins sometimes have difficulty in finding suitable conditions such as a convenient damp area in which to collect the mud, and this can delay breeding or even cause it to be abandoned for that season within a particular colony.

Once the outer walls are completed, the inside of the cup is then lined with vegetation and feathers, and even seaweed in some coastal colonies. With both members of the pair working together, the whole construction can take anything from one to two weeks to be completed. And all the time that familiar chattering sound can be heard overhead as the birds go about their business.

House martins are, of course, first cousins to swallows, which also patrol the cliffs here from time to time, often at a slightly lower level, looking for insects to take back to their young, probably at one of the nearby farms. They are slightly smaller than swallows, and their distinctively forked tails lack the long tail streamers sported by the adults of their larger cousins.

House martins make up for that with the bright white rump which shows up at remarkable distances in flight. They also have one other curious feature that sets them apart from all other small birds - the passerines - that breed in Europe: their legs are entirely feathered right down to their toes, the reasons for which are not entirely clear.

Although house martins often return to the same colony in successive years, they frequently change partners, and may also do so between the first and second broods, though this is probably due to failure of the first brood. Occasionally they may form a mixed pair with swallows. There is also one documented case of a house martin hybridizing with a sand martin, which must have been an interesting alliance as the latter species nest in burrows!

Young house martins, when they first leave the nest after about a month, coaxed out by their parents, are rather duller of plumage, browner and more freckled, though it is surprising how brown are the wings of adult birds when you see them still for a while. As these young are learning to use their wings properly, they continue to be fed by their parents for a few days and will return to the nest at night to roost. But soon the adults may be starting another clutch of 3-5 eggs which require incubating for approximately two weeks.

By the time this brood hatches, those from the first brood will be proficient flyers, and while a proportion of them will leave the colony altogether, some individuals have been observed helping to feed this next edition of brothers and sisters. House martins usually return to us later than swallows in spring, and tend to stay later at the back end of the year. But as autumn spreads its cooling fingers across coast and country, so they will form large pre-migration flocks in readiness for the long journey south.

We know very little about the exact places in Africa that our populations of house martins go to for the winter; very few British ringed birds have ever been found down there, possibly because the feathered legs of any dead birds that are found hide the individually-numbered metal rings, placed there by licensed bird ringers, that will subsequently yield so much useful information.

But leave our shores they surely will for another year and with the now fledged young kittiwakes and fulmars abandoning the breeding site also, the cliffs in the vicinity of Cullernose Point become strangely quiet until the year goes full circle and they will once more ring out to the sounds of the seabirds and their unlikely neighbours.

*A*UGUST

INSECT MISCELLANY

Walking along the coastal dunes during August can produce quite a variety of insects, some spectacular, some more inconspicuous, some identified, others for ever remaining a mystery, and many overlooked completely, but all part of that huge order of six-legged invertebrates that appeal to some of us more than others.

Butterflies are one of the most obvious and outstanding groups of insects, their bright iridescence enhanced on bright days by the sun's rays. Some summers one or two species stand out as being very common, another summer another species will make its presence felt more frequently. Thus, in our gardens, the summer of 1991 seemed to be the year of the large white, while the small tortoiseshell - surely one of our most familiar and versatile butterflies occurring in a wide range of habitats - along with its near relatives, the peacock and the red admiral, were conspicuous by their scarcity or even absence, though the red admiral made up for this in 1992. But on the dunes, meadow browns and common blues can often be relied on to make up for these shortfalls.

Laying their eggs on plants of the pea family, most often birdsfoot trefoil, but also restharrow, clover, black medick and others, the colourful common blue butterflies can be less conspicuous when resting head down on a stem of marram grass, perhaps with wings closed, when the more spotted pattern of the underwing takes over. Or you may come across a pair quietly mating close by the foodplants, when the more subtle colouring of the female can be studied.

But a male common blue in flight, with its brilliant blue wings edged with white, can not only steal the show, but also lead you a merry dance as it flits round you in erratic fashion.

Try following it, and you will soon lose the trail, sometimes right under your nose! Just as you have given up, it, or another individual, will appear in front of you and set you off again. The females are altogether a more subtle edition, usually browner, though some occur in a bluer form.

A walk through the dunes will also produce countless meadow browns, dull by comparison with the common blues, but an attractive butterfly nevertheless.

For once, the females are brighter, males being quite a dark brown with a subdued false eye on the upper forewings. The female has one too, but hers is encased in an orange surround on her otherwise pale brown wings.

These false eyes not infrequently save butterflies from becoming breakfast for a bird, which, in going for the 'eye', makes the mistake of aiming for the false one, causing the butterfly only to lose a small part of its wing instead of its life.

The meadow brown is said to be Britain's commonest butterfly and must suffer from the 'starling syndrome' of human complacency towards it in the face of success.

In some years we get invasions of less common butterflies coming here from the continent, such as the painted lady, which to my eye resembles a washed-out version of a small tortoiseshell. In 1992 clouded yellows reached as far north as Northumberland in small numbers for those lucky enough to see them. So it is always worth keeping an eye out for unusual visitors.

Think of moths and you think of their night-time activities, but not all moths are nocturnal. In fact, there are some very spectacular day-flying ones, and Holy Island is again, though perhaps unexpectedly, a good place to see one of them - the garden tiger moth. Their 'woolly bear' caterpillars are often a familiar sight to people walking in the dunes in late summer before hibernation, or when they re-emerge in spring. The adult moths appearing in July and August are extremely spectacular with the so-called brown and cream 'tiger' pattern on the upperwings, while the underwing is a bright orangey-red with dark spots, designed to warn off predators. A close view will also reveal red hairs at the back of its head.

While the majority of six-spot burnet moths show themselves in July, there are usually a few late ones to be seen as the month turns. Black with prominent red spots on the upperwing, this exhibits a green sheen in the sunlight. They also possess large hairy antennae, visible as they cluster together on the flowers of lesser knapweed or, perhaps more discerningly, on the flowerheads of pyramidal orchids with which they almost clash!

They do cause confusion also, because at the same time as the adult burnet moths are on the wing, the caterpillars of another red and black moth are devouring the final remnants of ragwort leaves before spinning a silken cocoon just underground in which to spend the winter. These are the caterpillars of the cinnabar moth, the adults of which fly earlier in the year, around May and June. Displaying yellow and black bodies, these caterpillars are an excellent example of 'warning colouration' since they are distasteful to birds.

Indeed, their main foodplant of ragwort is itself poisonous and the caterpillars absorb some of the toxins as protection. So they are able to flaunt themselves very publicly without fear of hungry beaks grabbing them. Any bird foolish enough to try them for a meal soon learns an unpleasant lesson.

Watching butterflies can be a frustrating experience, especially if you are trying to follow them through a pair of binoculars to get a better view. With such a rapid and often erratic flight, you are frequently left wondering just where your subject has disappeared to. Also it can be difficult to see true colours on a moving butterfly; you really need to find a resting one to appreciate its true beauty. But just casually watching butterflies moving over and into the surrounding vegetation on a warm summer's day, is a sight that brings pleasure to many people.

Sadly many butterflies are becoming quite scarce now, in large part through loss of habitat and suitable foodplants for the caterpillars, but they are fascinating creatures, different species having individually different lifestyles. Our countryside and coast without butterflies, would certainly be much the poorer.

SEPTEMBER

ON THE ROCKS

As the ebbing tide rolls out the causeway once again, St. Mary's Island relinquishes its island status for a few more hours. On some neap tides, the causeway is never covered at all and the steady tramp of feet continues during high tide as visitors make their way across to explore this breath of Tyneside.

But on spring tides, the causeway is cut off for up to four hours and the creatures of the deep can go about their business for a longer spell. Towards the end of September the equinoctial tides ebb far out, and one of the exciting things to do, after you have checked your tidetable carefully, is to follow it out and explore the rocks and pools low down on the shore that rarely give up their secrets.

So it was that I found myself, on a bright sunny morning with just a hint of breeze, at the end of September, bucket and net in hand, doing just such a thing. Three hours before the tide was due to turn, the causeway was well uncovered and the wading birds, moving in to spend the winter on our coast, were spread about the seaweed-covered rocks, making the most of their feeding time before the rising tide committed them to a few hours roosting in the adjacent fields.

High up on the shore the seaweeds lie brittle on the rocks, the buoying bladders of these wracks redundant until the tide returns. One of my favourites - egg or knotted wrack - has a single large egg-shaped bladder in the centre of its stem and displays the most wonderful range of yellows and browns, so that an alighting turn stone, that most

harlequin of wading birds, melts in among the blending hues. Alongside it are both flat and bladder wrack, while some green *Enteromorpha* seaweeds cling to the rounded boulders. A few limpets their make home on the side of this concrete walkway.

Once past the lighthouse, with its excellent information centre and shop, you can go down onto what I call the real rocks. Caution is the password; sloping seaweed covered rocks can be lethal and should be treated with great respect. One false step and you could be accidentally joining the very creatures you have come to see.

Limpets are everywhere. Each limpet has its own 'home' on the rock, to the extent that each time it returns as the tide ebbs, it must even face exactly the same way so that the fit is perfect. On hard rocks, the limpet will grind the bottom of its shell to match the shape of its chosen spot, but on soft rocks, the strategy is reversed to match its needs.

It then clamps itself on, retaining a little layer of moisture so that the biggest enemy of many of these creatures does not take its toll - desiccation. Remove a limpet from its rock and you have virtually signed its death warrant for it will be unable to relocate home in this unnatural situation.

On the more sheltered side of rocks the limpets can afford to have taller shells, whereas on the weather side, flatness ensures survival as the big breakers crash and gurgle in the gullies. Some limpets are so high up the beach that for several days on end during the neap tides, they may never be covered by water and therefore unable to wander off and feed on the surrounding algae which they rasp from the rocks.

As you travel down the shore, the number of acorn barnacles cemented to the rocks increases noticeably. Adaptable crustaceans, they can live across a wide area of the beach from high up to low down. Only able to feed when covered by water, by opening their trap doors and literally kicking their legs out to filter food from the passing currents, those lower down the shore therefore have the edge as it were over their higher relatives and grow more quickly. Able to reproduce in a year, their lives are entirely speeded up and they succumb at about three!

For those higher up, life is more leisurely; breeding does not occur until they are three and they may subsequently reach the ripe old age of five years if their main predator, the dog whelk, does not find them first. Most of the dog whelks here appeared to be clustered on barnacles fairly low down the shore.

On St. Mary's Island, with a number of the big rocks dropping vertically for several metres, there is the opportunity to observe creatures that normally only occur in quite deep water, alongside those one is more familiar with. Thus it was that as I clambered underneath a large overhanging rock to look at the hundred or more beadlet sea anemones sheltering on the underside I noticed in the bottom of the gully three dahlia anemones, characteristically covered with small particles of grit. As I got my eye in for them, I noticed several more in adjoining gullies, and was fortunate enough, via various contortions of my body, to actually see one still covered by water and thus showing the full extent of its beauty as its tentacles waited in anticipation of a passing meal.

Also on the underside of these rocks there were good coverings of the green breadcrumb sponge, and little yellow purse sponges hanging in amongst a colony of red sea squirts. A gentle pressure on these lets you know how they get their name as a little jet of water is expelled.

Stopping by a water-filled gully in the rocks for a bite of lunch, I was now far enough down the beach for the big brown kelp seaweeds to be growing. Only at home in deep water, these oarweeds can grow to several metres high. But here they were not so tall, their holdfasts clinging to the side of the rock. Sitting still, I noticed a large shore crab, probably male by its size, gently making its way along the bottom, while my eye then caught sight of another crab, this time a hermit crab gently using its front pincers to manipulate an item of food, as the back legs, hidden from view, help the animal to keep company with its borrowed home, in this case, the shell of an edible winkle.

As the crab grows, however, it has to seek out new and bigger shells in which to live, and in some cases may share these with a species of worm, or even have a sea anemone hitching a lift on the roof. As the tide continued to recede, so beds of mussels appeared. They were only small specimens, but clustered together in groups, all with their shells tightly closed to overcome the few vulnerable hours when they would be exposed.

The mussel is another creature that is subjected to the attentions of predatory dog whelks - the carnivores of the beach - though I did not see any on these particular ones. Those dog whelks that feed on these bivalves - that is two-part shells, each side being a mirror image of the other - tend to show a blue tinge in their shells, whereas those that specialise in the white-shelled barnacles, themselves have whitish shells.

They have a clever way of piercing the shell in the form of a siphon that is used in the way a joiner uses a bradawl, making a neat round hole in the shell through which chemicals are pumped to break the body down to a more liquid form that can be sucked out.

Finally when the tide was just about at 'rock bottom' a new kind of seaweed appeared, swirling into a myriad pattern on the water surface. This is the thong weed; long brown straps, flattened laterally, and no more than half an inch wide, that emanate from buttons at the base. Gradually the sea gave it up to leave it lying on the rocks in long leathery strands before the tide turned and re-embraced it.

Seaweeds lying on the rocks during low tide have an important function, particularly those with broad fronds and thick growth. While, on hot sunny days, the upper surface of the seaweed may become dry and brittle, underneath it retains a dampness and an almost slimy texture, and it is here that many vulnerable creatures - winkles, topshells, small crabs - seek shelter from the drying effects of the sun.

So turning over seaweeds to see what is underneath is fine so long as they are placed back again afterwards. The same goes for small boulders in rockpools which often have interesting passengers on their undersides. They like to be carefully returned to their original positions, especially those that can barely or only slowly move.

In the pools here, the undersides of a couple of pebbles in a rockpool revealed firstly a coat of mail shell - that relative of the limpet that exhibits a shell in eight sections all fitting together like the armour-plating of knights of old.

A topshell, a marine snail so called from its resemblance to the spinning tops that children of my generation used to be enthralled by, fell off and back into the pool. These snails are well able to cope with being knocked off their rocks, often by a big wave breaking at the very point and dislodging them. They have a little horny front door, properly called an operculum, which safely shuts the creature inside its shell as it is swirled around in the waves. Once a more sheltered spot is detected, the door is opened and the creature can go about its business once more. The shell of this creature, when washed up empty on the beach, often reveals the beautiful middle layer of mother-of-pearl that goes to help make its protective home.

Another rock had on its underside a black scale worm that wriggled its way along before I replaced it in the pool. These creatures really need a magnifying glass to reveal their true splendour of overlapping scales, and a line of guard hairs along the side of the body.

So finally the tide had given up all the secrets it was going to, and turned to start the whole cycle off again. As it did, I was able to stand on a rock momentarily and look down through the clear water to see the kelps fully extended upwards in the gently swaying water of a sheltered inlet. So often only those among us who are divers can enjoy these forests of seaweed that rise up with the rising tide. But briefly, every so often, that which is mostly hidden by the water is visible for us landlubbers to look at and appreciate. It is a special moment.

OCTOBER

ARCTIC VISITORS

Autumn is an exciting time of year on the coast for birdwatchers: not only does it bring the prospect of scarce migrant birds but it is also the time when our more regular winter visitors from breeding grounds far to the north and east start arriving on the coast to swell the numbers of those already here.

Wading birds slip in quietly and space themselves out along the shoreline while overhead the calling of geese announces their arrival. Some stay with us through the winter months, others just use it as a 'filling station' before moving on to their particular chosen location. With many wildfowl these places are often traditional.

So it is that part, sometimes perhaps all, of the brent geese breeding on the Spitsbergen archipelago, high above the Arctic Circle, choose to spend the winter months on the National Nature Reserve at Lindisfarne, which stretches from Budle Bay in the south to Cheswick Black Rocks in the north and includes part of Holy Island. Here they are under the total protection of English Nature, whose wardens make regular winter counts to closely monitor this unique population.

At Fenham Flats, on the mainland side of the reserve, they can often be seen strung out in long lines at the water's edge. Or alternatively you may glimpse them from the causeway as you make your way across to Holy Island. These aggregations can be noisy with very frequent domestic bickering and the occasional short flights to another

part of the group. And yet at other times it is surprising how inconspicuous they can be as they mingle among the large numbers of wigeon.

For brent are one of our smallest geese, buoyant on water, agile in flight. They also come in two shades - pale-bellied and dark-bellied - and breed in discreet populations; those breeding on Spitsbergen are of the pale-bellied race.

The history of wintering brent geese in Northumberland is an interesting one and is very much tied to their major food-plant - Zostera, otherwise known as eel-grass, our only marine underwater flowering plant. Over a century ago, the majority of brent geese wintering here were actually of the dark-bellied variety though there were probably a few pale ones among them.

Not only that, but their numbers greatly exceeded those of today; on 3rd March 1886, what was said to be the largest flock ever recorded in Britain - 30,000 birds - was apparently counted by that well-known wildfowler, Abel Chapman, during one of his wildfowling trips to the area. Though this was subsequently thought to have been a slight over-estimate, it was, nevertheless, exceptional, and must have been a thrilling sight.

Thereafter numbers began to decline rapidly until between 1931 and 1953 a maximum of only 500 was noted. This seemed to be linked to a decline in the eel-grass which also created a major distributional upheaval among the wintering birds. Nowadays, they are mostly pale-bellied and numbers have again increased; in early January 1993 a peak of 2,350 was counted.

For me, wintering wildfowl are very exciting. Watching them one winter's day as the incoming tide persuaded them to head for a different area of the reserve, a friend and I walked north along the shore from the mainland end of Holy Island causeway, which by that time was covered by water.

Huge flocks of knot were swirling round, dunlin fed urgently on the mud and a group of oystercatchers decided to rest up over the high tide period. But every so often a group of brents would fly past heading on out of sight. Eventually, after rounding several 'corners' ourselves, we came across them in a little inlet feeding among myriad waders and gulls that were concentrated in this still accessible area. Some were moving quickly over the mud which had a green sheen to it; it was obviously covered in eel-grass.

Yet others were swimming on the shallow water, necks stretched forward as they dipped their heads beneath the surface to come up with strands of vegetation hanging from their bills. It was obviously a productive high-tide feeding place. The light was good and most of them appeared to be pale-bellied birds but the odd one or two were of a darker hue. Occasionally more flew in to join them and it was probably the best view I had ever had of these geese.

But whenever I see these birds, perhaps arriving, perhaps departing, or just working their way through winter as these were, I am always led in my mind to that other part of their year on the breeding grounds. Many of the wintering birds here, including the brent geese, breed up in the high Arctic, itself an area of the world I find fascinating. So, when I had the opportunity to visit Spitsbergen in the summer of 1991, I jumped at the occasion for I would be able to fit another piece into the brent goose jigsaw.

Now it has to be said that not everyone goes all the way to Spitsbergen, less than 600 miles from the North Pole, with a sighting of brent geese at the top of their list when there are many other Arctic delights to enjoy. For here were several other birds that we *often only get a glimpse of in winter - glaucous gulls, grey phalaropes, and rarest of all, ivory gulls, alongside mammals that we never see like walrus, arctic fox and that king of the Arctic, the polar bear, known locally as the ice bear.*

But for me the brents were a major part of this whole exciting experience. And sure enough, after a few days, there were our first ones, some with fairly small young in tow. They were quite shy and did not allow a close approach, but that didn't matter. They were in spectacular surroundings, and some in company with barnacle geese, which themselves pass through Northumberland in autumn en route to their wintering grounds on the Solway Firth. It was like catching up with old friends.

We also came across some of the empty nests, still with their down feather linings and a few empty eggshells. Here, arctic skuas take some of the eggs, as do glaucous gulls occasionally, although they prefer to plunder the barnacles . Surprisingly the real predator of the brent geese is - yes - none other than the ice bear.

As soon as the young can fly at the end of the short Arctic summer, they leave Spitsbergen in family parties and perhaps stop over briefly on Bear Island before they head down the coast of northern Norway making for Denmark, where they make landfall in late August.

Here they used to utilise the Danish part of the Waddenzee, but in the last few years a major re-distribution seems to have taken place. It is thought likely that this is due, once again, to a decline in eel-grass, with a site on the Baltic coast and two in north-west Jutland now taking preference. Here a proportion of the population may spend the entire winter. But part of them head out over the North Sea for the final stage of the journey to Lindisfarne, the only British wintering area for this particular population.

At the beginning of the winter season, the brent geese on Lindisfarne tend to favour Enteromorpha, a common green alga that grows extensively along our coast. But as winter winds on, and the Enteromorpha disappears, so they turn more to the eel-grass. This, however, they have to share with the wigeon, which also arrive in spectacular numbers in some winters. But there are two different species of eel-grass at Lindisfarne and current research being undertaken by scientists from Durham University suggests that while the brents appear to concentrate on Zostera noltii, the wigeon favour Z. marina, thus avoiding competition. The average goose eats about 100 grams a day, adding up to 25 tonnes in a winter season.

Not surprisingly, therefore, that early into the New Year the food starts running short, and particularly if their brethren on the other side of the North Sea have been forced out from their wintering area by a freeze-up and have flown over to join up with those already here. So during January and February in most years, numbers start to decrease dramatically as the birds undertake the first step of their journey back to the Arctic.

But just which way are they all going? Intriguingly, during recent winters, increasing numbers of the brent geese present at Lindisfarne have again been dark-bellied birds from the western Siberian breeding population, which normally winters further south in England; 150 were counted here in the winter of 1992/93. In October 1975, a pale-bellied bird was noted in the wintering flock bearing a numbered neck collar which indicated that it had been marked at Bathurst Island in arctic Canada and since then one or two other Canadian ringed birds have been positively sighted, perhaps having overshot their main wintering area in Ireland.

It seems the brent goose jigsaw still has a few more pieces to be fitted in.

November

PUPPING TIME

The Farne Islands, owned by the National Trust and situated about a mile offshore from Bamburgh, are probably and justifiably best known for their vast breeding colonies of seabirds thronging the cliffs during the summer months, to the utter delight of visitors, many of whom have never witnessed the clamour and activity, not to mention the distinctive odour, of a seabird colony before. But the birds are not alone.

Grey seals can be seen around our coast right through the year, and are frequently encountered hauled up on the rocks near the Longstone during the summer, as they have been since the time of St. Cuthbert in the 7th century, taking to the water only when the boats come close. They are just as curious of the visitors as the visitors are of them, but feel a little more secure in their watery habitat than on land when a close encounter of the human kind seems imminent.

The larger of the two seals that breed in Britain, the other being the common, an adult male grey can weigh in at a solid 36 stone (230 kg.), making the females seem quite lightweight at a mere 23 and a half stone (150 kg.)! Common seals on average are about half that weight.

Of course their size should help you sort out the greys from the commons, but when they are in the water that may not be quite so easy. All is not lost, however, as the distinctive bits that you need to see are usually above the waterline, namely their heads!

Male grey seals are always said to have Roman noses, giving a convex profile if you see them sideways on; the females have flatter muzzles. Common seals, however, have a much more 'doggy' expression, but here in Northumberland, they tend to be the exception rather than the rule.

Another important distinction between the two is the timing of pupping. Common seal pups are born during June and July and can take to the water almost immediately. The reason for this is that the white first coat is moulted inside the mother before the pup is born, and therefore it arrives in the outside world already clad in its first adult dress. So they are much more advanced at birth than grey seal pups which are, in turn, born still in their white coats which adequately cover them, but which are not suitable to go to sea in.

Grey seals, then, through preference pup further up the beach out of reach of the high tides that could well wash such vulnerable creatures away; here they can safely stay until they moult out their white 'puppy' coats and look more like small sleek adults. With this knowledge in mind, it comes as a bit of a shock to discover the newly born grey seal pups on the Farnes sporting multi-coloured coats - at least that is the first impression as you approach in a boat! White blobs with pink, purple, green and yellow blotches are dotted across the beaches mainly of the North Wamses but also South Wamses and Northern Hares. But as the boat reduces speed a little way offshore and you are able to get a steadier and more extended view, it becomes apparent that each pup has just a single colour on it, and it is there for a good reason.

The wardens, who visit the pupping islands about every four days until the end of the breeding season, mark the pups in order to get an accurate count. So each week one of four colours is used to help keep the records straight. The colouring does not, of course, harm the pups, and their mothers, several of whom were lying up alongside them when I saw them, do not worry about this decoration; the all-important thing for them is to learn to recognise the individual smell of their own offspring when it is born in order to form the vital bond between them. In any case, when the pups shed their white coats, so their 'colour codes' go too! In 1992, the weekly counts came up with a final total of 985 pups born into a total population of approximately 3,500.

Once the pups are born, they begin to suckle their mothers who, at the start, are fat and round. Seal's milk is extremely rich, being almost 60% fat, and as the females do not themselves feed during the early part of lactation, which generally lasts in total for about eighteen days, so the fat is literally being transferred from one animal to the other; while the mother becomes a mere shadow of her former self, beside her lies her increasingly round and fat, torpedo-shaped offspring! At the end of lactation, however. she abandons her pup, which in the next few days loses its white natal coat and is then able to get its first experience of the truly marine life.

By the end of this period the mother must be completely exhausted but she is not yet free to leave the breeding beach and go back to sea to make up her lost reserves. While the females have been busy giving their young a good start in life, the males have been hanging around the colony as well. They also fast during this period but do not, of course, lose fat at the same rate as the females.

A few males are dominant and they will defend the prime spots in the colony, mainly by threatening rivals but only rarely resorting to outright battle. Once the females are relieved of feeding their offspring, so they come on heat and the males will mate with them; one male may mate with as many as ten females, while others are excluded altogether. But the females themselves may be mated by up to three different males. Then, and only then, do the females get away out to sea.

Implantation of the egg does not take place, however, until the following spring, after the female has herself moulted at the beginning of the year. Females do not become sexually mature until they are between three and five years old, and while males can be sexually mature at about six, it will be another few years before they are able to achieve a position of dominance in the hierarchy. So when you see them bobbing round your boat as you visit the Farnes in summer, most of the adult females will be pregnant, and the males will probably already be making their individual presences felt among their rivals.

The grey seals around the Farnes are in many respects fortunate. Their traditional pupping beaches are relatively large and sheltered, and, although they may not entirely appreciate it, they are well looked after and protected during the pupping season under the watchful eyes of the National Trust. Although seals may not be everyone's friend, they are highly popular with the boat-borne visitors and great ambassadors for conservation in their world-famous sanctuary off the Northumberland coast.

DECEMBER

A FISHY TALE

Here in Northumberland we are fortunate indeed to have some lovely rivers, several with names to match their beauty: where else could there be a River Coquet? The Tweed sounds good and solid while the Aln becomes a real tongue twister for visitors.

We walk beside them, we watch the wildlife that lives alongside them, we admire the bankside flowers, but, unless we go fishing, how often do we think of what goes on under the surface of the water?

Right through the year there is a private world going on down there, from which we occasionally get clues but are seldom privileged to witness the complete picture. But at the back end of the year a fishy tale starts unfolding for the umpteenth time, as the adult sea trout are returning to their natal rivers to spawn.

As you walk alongside the river Aln on a crisp, calm December morning, bankside trees reflected on the calm surface, there is little hint of the frantic activity going on below, save for the occasional ripple as a fish breaks the surface. But on the gravelly bottom of the clear shallow part of the river, a female sea trout is frantically contorting her tail end to gouge out a 'redd' in which to deposit her eggs.

Although fish may return to their river at any time during the year, a lot come back during late autumn. Should the river be too low in water, they may wait offshore for a run of floodwater. When all seems suitable they will move in, mostly at night. Those returning early in the year may hardly feed until spawning time, by which time they will have used up vital stores of energy and will be less fit; it stands to reason, therefore, that the later-running ones tend to be in better condition with plenty of energy reserves stored in that streamlined scaly form. But how do they know which river to enter? It seems that each river has its own distinctive smell learnt at birth; marking individuals has shown that very few ever go back up the wrong one!

Lesbury, about a couple of miles upstream from the Aln estuary, is the first suitable spawning place in this river, but other fish will spread themselves out further upstream. To encourage them to move on up the river, a fish pass has been provided beside the rather formidable-looking weir, down which a good run of white water rushes. The noise of this encourages the fish to move over to that side of the river and thus their onward passage receives a 'step-up' as it were.

But it doesn't always work! A later-running female may come across what seems to her a highly suitable place below the weir to lay her eggs, and in moving the gravel to shape her own 'redd' may inadvertently destroy those eggs deposited by an earlier female! The lost eggs will not be wasted; they may provide a good meal for a dipper.

The amount of eggs laid by individual females is directly linked to body size; a good rule of thumb is about 500 eggs per kilo of body weight. It stands to reason then that a first time breeder, weighing in at only about 1 kilo, will lay between 500 and 700 eggs, whereas older ones, which may reach 10 kilos, will lay ten times as many. Once a female has spawned, she is known as a kelt.

When all the eggs are deposited on the river bed, they are covered up with surrounding gravel by their parents. If all goes according to plan they will hatch out the following March or April. But there are hazards waiting for the young right from the moment they squirm out of the egg: many hungry mouths waiting for a good meal, and a hundred or so smolts would go a long way to satisfying some pangs of hunger.

For those that do make it, more by good luck than good judgement, they will stay in the river right through their year of hatching and into early summer of the following year. During this time they will grow only slowly, less than a centimetre a month.

But now smoltification takes place and an extraordinary thing happens. Not all the young born to the same two adult sea trout will themselves go to sea; rather they will spend their entire lives in the river. Thus they will mature and breed themselves as river trout, but a large proportion of their progeny will enter the sea and themselves become sea trout. What exactly decides this factor is uncertain, but it seems to be linked to their genetic make-up.

For the majority that do go to sea, however, a new stage in their lives now begins. Before they can enter the salt water, their bodies have to internally adapt to a marine existence and an intake of much richer food. As they leave our north-east rivers, so they turn right and head down the coast towards that bulge of England that forms East Anglia. Here they join up with large numbers of their kith and kin born in other rivers and grow rapidly on a high-energy diet that consists largely of sandeels.

After their first full year at sea, some may start the northward journey back to their river, while others may continue to grow bigger in that sea area for anything up to four years more. Whenever they choose, they will encounter hazards on the way. For those returning to the Northumbrian rivers before the end of August, they may encounter those flat-bottomed boats unique to this part of the British coast - cobles - waiting with their T-shaped nets set to catch the fish as they hug the coastline seeking that distinctive scent of 'their' river. Until the end of October, the rod and line fishermen are ready on the riverbank to make the catch of a lifetime.

But for those that make it all the way, the cycle has come full circle. The more aggressive males not only fend off lesser males while waiting for the females to arrive, but having fertilised one batch of eggs, may then seek out other females. Thus some of the more successful males may completely burn themselves out as they move around the local area and then the smaller males may get their chance. But the females, unlike their close cousins the salmon, do not succumb once they have spawned, but live to see another year, maybe several more years.

We see little of this as we walk along the river. But next time you take a stroll down the river bank, keep an eye out for any telltale clues to what may be going on beneath the surface.

WHERE TO SEE SOME OF THE WILDLIFE MENTIONED

Red squirrels *may be encountered in any number of places, particularly early in the year, but perhaps you may be more lucky at Bolam Lake Country Park, the Forest Enterprise car parks of Thrunton Woods and Simonside, or the National Trust's properties at Cragside and Wallington Hall.*

Smew *and other sawbills are most likely to occur in winter on the Druridge Bay reserves or Holywell Pond, or Big Waters at Wideopen as well as some other freshwater lakes.*

Toads *go to spawning ponds in early spring all over the county. At Alnmouth they spawn in the marsh, at Druridge Bay Country Park in the pond near the entrance, at Newton Pool and so on. Be careful not to tread on the toads or run them over when looking for them. If you pick the creatures up to help them across the road, make sure you are taking them in the direction they want to go!*

Cowslips *occur on many of the links along the coast around April-time. Don't forget it's illegal to dig them up and take them home!*

The Harthope is one of several valleys in the Cheviots, all part of the Northumberland National Park, and holding a wide variety of wildlife, including **adders** *during spring and summer. As long as you don't intimidate adders, they won't hurt you.*

During warm summer evenings **bats** *can be seen in a variety of habitats. For instance, Daubenton's may be seen hunting over the Coquet at places like Warkworth or*

WHERE TO SEE SOME OF THE WILDLIFE MENTIONED

Rothbury, while pipistrelles may be seen flying round in suburban areas, or you may come across other species along woodland rides.

__House martins__ nest extensively on the sides of houses in many of our towns and villages, on farm barns and other buildings, but they can be seen in a 'natural' site on the coast south of Cullernose Point, between Howick and Craster.

The extensive area of sand dunes along our coast provide plenty of areas where you may observe __butterflies__ during a large part of the year, but you may need to go no further than your own garden or school grounds to see many others.

One of the interesting things about the __rock pools__ along our coast, is that each beach produces something different to look at. Remember to put seaweed back as you found it, and to carefully replace boulders that you have turned over back as they were to prevent seashore creatures from overheating and drying out during low tide. Also check local tidetables carefully before venturing too far down a beach or you may get cut off by the incoming tide.

The best place to see __brent geese__ in winter is around Fenham Flats in the Lindisfarne National Nature Reserve between Budle Bay and Holy Island. Sometimes they can be seen in the harbour at Holy Island village.

Although __grey seals__ may be encountered anywhere along the coast right through the year, in autumn, their only pupping area in Northumberland is on the Farne Islands and occasional boat trips go out from Seahouses when the weather permits.

WHERE TO SEE SOME OF THE WILDLIFE MENTIONED

A walk along the River Aln upstream from Lesbury, or along most of our other major rivers, may, if you are lucky, give you a glimpse of **sea trout** *digging out their 'redds' to lay their eggs, but their presence may only be marked by the occasional ripple on the surface. If you are very lucky, you may see them 'jumping' up one of the fish ladders that have been put in place to help them upstream, but this is very unpredictable.*

Remember to respect the Country Code, and enjoy your wildlife watching!

FOLLOW THE COUNTRY CODE

Enjoy the countryside and respect its life and work.
Guard against all risk of fire.
Fasten all gates.
Keep your dogs under close control.
Keep to public paths across farmland.
Use gates and stiles to cross fences, hedges and walls.
Leave livestock, crops and machinery alone.
Take litter home.
Help to keep all water clean.
Protect wild life, plants and trees.
Take special care on country roads.
Make no unnecessary noise.

USEFUL ADDRESSES

Enquiries about Bats to either:
Hancock Museum, Newcastle. OR : English Nature

English Nature,
Archbold House,
Archbold Terrace,
Jesmond, Newcastle upon Tyne, NE2 1EG
Tel : 091 281 6316

Farne Islands Boatmen at Seahouses:
H.J. Hanvey Tel : 0665 720388
J.G. Mackay Tel : 0665 721144
Billy Shiel Tel : 0665 720308

Hancock Museum, Barras Bridge,
Newcastle upon Tyne, NE2 4PT

National Rivers Authority,
Eldon House, Gosforth,
Newcastle upon Tyne, NE3 3UD

National Trust,
Scots Gap, Morpeth,
Northumberland, NE61 4EG
Farne Islands Head Warden Tel : 0665 720651 Coastal Warden Tel : 0665 5763665

USEFUL ADDRESSES

Northumberland Countryside Department,
Northumberland County Council,
County Hall, Morpeth,
Northumberland, NE61 2EF

Northumberland National Park,
Northumberland County Council,
Eastburn, South Park,
Hexham, Northumberland, NE46 1BS

Northumberland Wildlife Trust,
Hancock Museum, Barras Bridge,
Newcastle upon Tyne, NE2 4PT

Royal Society for the Protection of Birds,
North of England Office,
'E' Floor, Milburn House,
Dean Street, Newcastle upon Tyne, NE1 1LE

'Watch' Group,
(Junior section of the Wildlife Trusts)
c/o Northumberland Wildlife Trust.

Young Ornithologists' Club,
c/o R.S.P.B. Newcastle Office.

SANDHILL PRESS PUBLICATIONS

THE BIGGEST MINING VILLAGE IN THE WORLD : a social history of Ashington

by Mike Kirkup

THE BODY IN THE BANK : famous Northern murders

Retold by Sandhill Press

A fascinating collection of murders, trials and subsequent harsh punishments.

CUSTOMS & TRADITIONS OF NORTHUMBRIA

Retold by Sandhill Press

Customs and traditions associated with ceremonies, seasons and times of the year, leisure and work.

THE GREAT GUNMAKER : the life of Lord Armstrong

by David Dougan

IN AND AROUND

ALNWICK...MORPETH...ROTHBURY...WARKWORTH

by Ian Smith

First in a new series in which Ian explores Northumberland's towns, villages and their rivers.

THE LAST YEARS OF A FRONTIER

by D.L. Tough

A history of the Borders during the turbulent times of Elizabeth I.

MYTH AND MAGIC OF NORTHUMBRIA

Retold by Sandhill Press

Wizards and witches, fairies and sprites, charms and spells from Northumbria's folklore.

NORTHUMBRIA IN PICTURES

A new revised edition of our successsful colour souvenir guide -
40 superb colour photographs and accompanying text.

NORTHUMBRIAN COASTLINE

by Ian Smith

A walker's guide from Berwick upon Tweed to North Shields printed in the author's own handwriting & including his many line drawings and maps.

THE NORTHUMBRIAN PUB : an architectural history

by Lynn F. Pearson

A social and architectural history of our north eastern pubs.

ROGUES AND REIVERS OF THE NORTH COUNTRY

Retold by Sandhill Press

Tales of highwaymen, smugglers, bodysnatchers and the Border Reivers.

UPPER COQUETDALE

by David Dippie Dixon

Northumberland : its history, traditions, folklore and scenery.

Originally published in 1903 - a special limited numbered edition.

VICTORIAN & EDWARDIAN NORTHUMBRIA

from old photographs

by J.W. Thompson & D. Bond

WARKWORTH

by Ian Smith

A charming guide to this unique Northumbrian village.

YORKSHIRE COASTLINE

by Ian Smith

A follow-up to the highly successful 'Northumbrian Coastline', this second guide covers the coast from the River Tees to Bridlington.